Luisa's LAB!

Judith Brand

Contents

Rigby®
A Harcourt Achieve Imprint

www.Rigby.com
1-800-531-5015

Sunday

At school, my class is learning about water.

I want to experiment with water at home.

I will observe what happens
and write it down.
My parents will take pictures
of me.

Monday

I put water into different things
that I found in the kitchen.
Water can fit the shape
of a muffin tin.

Water can also
fit the shape
of a mug.
I tipped the mug
and the water
ran out. Oops!

My dog, Lily, helped me clean up the spill!

I learned that water is a liquid. It can change shape.

Tuesday

(3:30 p.m.)

I put ice in
the muffin tin.
It doesn't fit
the shape.

Ice doesn't
fit the shape
of the mug,
either.

6

If I tip the mug, the ice doesn't run out.

Lily loves ice and wants to eat some!

I learned that ice is a solid. It keeps its shape.

I put water
in a dish
and put it outside
in the freezing cold.

When I checked the dish,
there was some water and ice.
Later it was all ice! Wow!

WOW!

8

Brrr! Lily and I were cold!

I learned that water
freezes at 32°F
and it turns into ice.

Wednesday

Some treats
are ice, too!
Mom gave me a recipe
and we made them together.

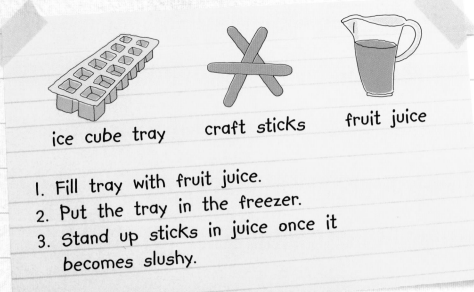

ice cube tray   craft sticks   fruit juice

1. Fill tray with fruit juice.
2. Put the tray in the freezer.
3. Stand up sticks in juice once it
   becomes slushy.

10

The treats were finally ready! Yum!

5:00 p.m.

My mom helped me heat some water on the stove.

I had to wait, but the water finally started to boil.

I learned that water
turns to steam
when it is heated.

what I Learned

Water is a liquid.
It can change shape.

Ice is a solid.
It does not change shape.

Water freezes
when it is very cold.

Water turns to steam
when it is very hot.

My dog, Lily, likes water
and ice!

Glossary

Boil to heat water until it turns to steam

Freeze to cool water until it turns to ice

Liquid something that does not have a definite shape

Solid something that has a definite shape

Steam a cloud of tiny, hot water drops